Presented to

Sajeev. C

By

James, Gloria + Jordan

On This Date

Sept · 16/2000

Quiet Whispers From God's Heart

FOR MEN

STEVE FARRAR

COUNTRYMAN

I f I'd been choosing the title for this book, I wouldn't have chosen a phrase like *Whispers for Men*. I would have suggested *Two-by-Four's for Men*. It seems to me that it usually takes a two-by-four across the side of my head for God to get my attention.

But before God ever takes out the two-by-four, He *whispers*. He speaks gently. He speaks quietly. Yet we're usually so busy and so preoccupied that we don't hear. Or to be more precise, we hear but we don't listen.

Part of growing in our Christian walk is learning to hear God when He whispers. And life is certainly much easier when we respond to a whisper rather than something more severe.

Gradually, I'm learning to hear God's whispers. Hopefully, as I grow older, I'm growing more teachable. And it's the teachable man who responds to God's whispers.

I invite you to join me on the journey.

STEVE FARRAR

June 1999

CONTENTS

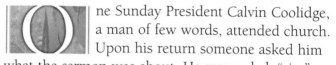
One Sunday President Calvin Coolidge, a man of few words, attended church. Upon his return someone asked him what the sermon was about. He responded, "sin."

"Well, what did the preacher say about it?"

"He said he's against it," replied Coolidge.

Sounds like a good idea. Especially in our day.

I once heard about a lady who justified her multiple affairs by remarking, "You have *your* sin, and I have *mine* . . ."

Really now. Do we all have our sin?

No.

In fact, I'm going to assert something radical. No Christian can live with sin—day in and day out, year in and year out, without even the slightest change or attempt to stop—and remain a Christian! Christianity without any change in behavior over the long haul is synthetic Christianity. Either we go to God in repentance and turn away from our sin, or we give over to sin.

The truth of the matter is, you need to be *afraid* of sin. You have to treat it as more deadly than a rattlesnake. That means you never dally with it.

You play with fire, you get burned. You mess with a snake, you get bit. You dabble in sin, you slide down the slippery slope that separates from God. There is nothing more dangerous than accepting and excusing sin—sin that has the power to cast into hell.

The enemy of our souls wants to destroy us. The Bible says that Satan goes around like a roaring lion trying to "devour" us (1 Pet. 5:8). Pick up today's paper and you can read about his successes. Tune into the latest church gossip, and hear of his latest victims.

As we walk through life we need to follow the Appalachian warning about river trails: *NEVER stop watching for rattlers!* We've got to be alert. Be on our guard. Because sin can creep up on us when we least expect it.

And when it does, we need to nip it in the bud before it becomes serious. We need to root it out, while it's only a half-formed thought—before it's been said . . . before it's been done.

How do you stay away from sin?

It's simple.

Stay as close to Christ as you possibly can.

Don't touch sin with a ten-foot pole. And if you do, deal with it immediately!

Stay in God's Word. Read it. Digest it. Memorize it.

You'd probably heard the cliché. *Either the Bible will keep you from sin or sin will keep you from the Bible.*

It's true.

> One reason sin flourishes is that it is treated like a cream puff instead of a rattlesnake.
>
> BILLY SUNDAY

once heard a story about a fellow named Henry Peterson, a fourth-string halfback on the University of Alabama football team. Henry was so low on the depth chart that he only played a few downs during mop-up time. These were the glory years of Coach Paul "Bear" Bryant, the most winning college football coach of his era.

Alabama's huge rivalry game every year was the season-ending intrastate battle with the University of Auburn Tigers. A few days before kickoff, Henry received a phone call from home: his father had died unexpectedly. Henry called Coach Bryant and said, "Coach, I can't be there for the game Saturday. You see, my father just died, and I need to go home."

Bear Bryant, who was in the midst of pregame preparations, felt sorry for the young man. "Son, don't you give this ball team another thought. You go home and be with your family. They need you."

"Thank you, Coach. I knew you would understand."

Sometime after returning home, Henry felt he had to return to Tuscaloosa and suit up for the Alabama-Auburn football game. On the day before the big game, he called Coach Bryant a second time.

"Coach, I've been thinking about it, and I can't let the team down. I'll be there Saturday afternoon."

Coach Bryant knew the young man deserved to be with his family during their time of grief. "No, it's not a problem if you're not at the game. You can stay home this weekend."

"No, Sir, I'll be there."

Two hours before the Alabama-Auburn kickoff, Henry found Coach Bryant in his office. The young man sat down before the coach and with as much earnestness as he could muster, he said, "Coach, I want you to start me today."

Coach Bryant looked up from his notes, not sure if he had heard right. "Henry, this is the Alabama-Auburn football game. I can't start you today. You've never started a football game in Alabama history."

"I know Coach. But you've *got* to start me today!" he persisted.

"All right, Henry, here's what we're going to do. I'm going to put you in on the first series of downs. The first time you hurt the Alabama football team, I'm pulling you out. Do you understand me?"

"Yes, Sir."

What would possess a fourth-string halfback to insist the coach start him in the biggest game of the season? Why would a legendary coach give his assent?

Both parties must have felt something in their gut—the same feeling that caused Gideon to trust God when the Lord said, "You don't need 10,000 men to defeat the Midianites, you only need three hundred. You can send everyone else home!" Gideon obeyed and destroyed the Midian army in a matter of hours.

Bear Bryant didn't send the rest of the football team home that afternoon, but he did let Henry Peterson run wild. The benchwarmer ran circles around the Auburn defense, scoring four touchdowns

in the first half. At halftime, Coach Bryant found Henry in the locker room.

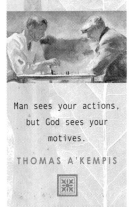

Man sees your actions, but God sees your motives.

THOMAS A'KEMPIS

"Henry, I don't know whether to kiss you or kill you. You've been sitting my bench for four years. Why didn't you tell me you knew how to play football like that?"

"Coach," the young man replied, "did you ever see me walking arm in arm with my daddy throughout this campus? Talking to him about the buildings and telling him what was going on around campus?"

Bear Bryant searched his brain. "Yes, I do believe I saw you with your father once or twice."

"Coach, my daddy was blind. Today was the first day he ever got to see me play football!"

One thing is for sure. Every one of us who names the name of Christ is "playing the game" before the eyes of our Heavenly Father. Proverbs 15:3 states it clearly: "The eyes of the Lord are in every place, keeping watch on the evil and the good."

He sees what we do in public, and He sees what we do in private. And when you realize that His eye is always upon you, you have a powerful motivation to live life to the very best of your ability.

He's watching you at work, and He's watching you at home.

What an opportunity to give Him your very best.

Bob enjoyed nothing better than driving from one garage sale to another on Saturday mornings. He never knew what treasure he might find sifting through other people's trash, especially in the Los Angeles suburb where he lived.

One Saturday morning, he spotted an old Harley-Davidson motorcycle parked in the garage, partially covered by a tattered quilt. The Harley wasn't part of the garage sale, but Bob asked if it was available anyway.

"Could be," the man behind the card-table replied. "The wife says everything has to go anyway. But I gotta tell you, the bike hasn't run since I got it. Motor seized up."

"Okay, so it's not working. What do you want for it?" Bob persisted.

"Oh, I don't know. How does thirty-five dollars sound?"

"Sold," he said. "Can I pick it up tomorrow?"

"Sure enough."

The rusty Harley sat in a corner of Bob's garage, merely taking up space for several weeks before he got around to calling the local Harley-Davidson dealership. He was connected to the parts department.

After describing his problem, the parts man asked for the motorcycle's serial number.

Bob rattled off the long number and then was put on hold.

When the parts man came back on, he said, "Uh, I'm going to have to call you back, okay? Can you give me a couple of days?"

"Sure."

The phone rang two days later, but this time a Harley executive was on the line. He struck Bob as being overly solicitous.

Better rich in God than rich in gold.

ANONYMOUS

"Listen, Bob, can you do something for me?"

"I can certainly try."

"I want you to take the seat off your bike and see if anything is written underneath. I'll wait right here for you."

Bob took a screwdriver and did as he was told. He lifted up the seat and noticed someone had engraved THE KING into the metal shell.

"It says THE KING," Bob reported.

For the longest time, the Harley executive didn't say anything.

"Bob, my boss has authorized me to offer you $300,000 for the bike, payable immediately. Would you like to sell it?"

Bob was so stunned he didn't know how to respond. He mumbled something about having to think about it and then slumped to the floor, wondering what he had done to deserve this.

The next day Jay Leno, the host of the "Tonight Show," called Bob, saying he had heard that he had a Harley-Davidson for sale. Explaining that he was a Harley collector, Leno offered Bob $500,000.

Why so much money? Because the bike belonged at one time to the King of Rock n' Roll, Elvis Presley.

The bike Bob had purchased on a whim for thirty-five dollars was worth half-a-million dollars!

We don't know it, but when we say yes to Christ, we belong to the *real* King, the King of the Universe, the Lord of all things. Did you know that you are worth far, far more than you ever imagined?

You see, we have Jesus Christ engraved on our souls, and we won't understand how much that is worth—or how undeserving we are—until we stand in His presence.

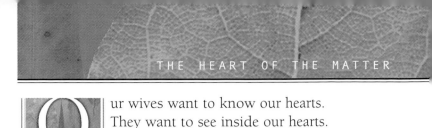

ur wives want to know our hearts. They want to see inside our hearts. They know that marriage is a heart-to-heart relationship. That's why good marriages wrap their hearts in Glad Wrap instead of Reynolds Wrap. Allow me to illustrate.

Let's say that we've had a party at our house: a great time with great food. About 3:00 a.m., I awake to a craving that whispers, "Guacomole . . . guacomole . . ." I make my way to the kitchen. All I want is just one more taste of guacomole dip and I'll go right back to sleep. Unfortunately, as I open the refrigerator door, I notice that all of the leftovers are wrapped in Reynolds Wrap—aluminum foil. So which container has the guacomole?

I take out the first container and open it. Peaches. I reach for another container. Carrot sticks. But I don't want carrot sticks. So I'm starting to get really frustrated. Finally, after I pull out five containers and have Reynolds Wrap scattered all over the kitchen, I find the guacomole.

Let's change the scenario.

I heed my late night craving and quietly make my way to the darkened kitchen. I open the refrigerator door and discover that the guacomole has been wrapped in Glad Wrap—plastic wrap. That makes me glad. Why does it make my glad? Because I can see through Glad Wrap! Glad Wrap is transparent. I don't have to guess what's inside! I can *see* what's inside!

Knit your hearts with
an unslipping knot.

WILLIAM
SHAKESPEARE

Good marriages are made up of two people who wrap their hearts in Glad Wrap. When your heart is wrapped in Glad Wrap, there's no mystery about what's in your heart.

A number of years ago, a man called me at home for help with a difficult situation. He had recently started to attend a church where he had been falsely accused of a terrible wrong and now was in danger of losing his marriage. Over the next few days I gave up much valuable time from an extremely tight schedule to meet with him, only to discover in the end that he had lied to me about the whole thing.

That night at dinner, when my five-year-old son spilled his apple juice, I went ballistic! Was I mad at my five-year-old? No. I was mad at the guy who had lied to me and wasted my time. It's called displaced anger. And I had taken mine out on an innocent five-year-old.

Later that night, Mary asked me how my day had gone.

"Fine," I replied.

She knew it *hadn't* gone fine.

So she asked me a few more questions and got a few more one-word answers.

Finally, I told her what had happened, and she understood. She knew I wasn't mad at my son for spilling his juice. She knew there was more in my heart than apple juice. But in order for her to understand, I had to take off the Reynolds Wrap and let her see what was going on inside.

I'd like to recommend that you do the same. Take the Reynolds Wrap off your heart and give the Glad Wrap a shot.

Trust me. It works.

And it will improve your marriage.

Sometimes godly men can't work out their differences. This shouldn't be a way of life. It wasn't a pattern with Paul, and it wasn't a pattern with Barnabas. Neither of them had a trail of broken relationships. When conflict came up in their relationship, 99 percent of the time they would resolve it and move on. But not this time. They talked, they prayed, and I imagine they even raised their voices . . . but they couldn't work it out. After years of friendship and ministry, they had come to an impasse (Acts 15:36-41).

Both men had strong feelings about John Mark. Very strong feelings. The Greek indicates that they were "strongly provoked." John Mark had deserted them in Pamphylia and headed back for Jerusalem (Acts 13:13). We don't know what caused him to leave, but when Barnabas suggested giving him another chance to minister, Paul just couldn't see it. I imagine he felt betrayed.

Barnabas was known in the early church as an encourager. That was his gift, his bent. Yes, it was true that young John Mark had abandoned his post, but Barnabas felt the young man had learned his lesson and deserved another opportunity to prove himself. And there was one other issue. Barnabas and John Mark were cousins (Col. 4:10), and blood runs thicker than water. To Paul, it made absolutely no sense. As hard as Barnabas tried to reason with him, Paul just couldn't see it. So they decided to take different paths.

If you've ever seen two rams butt heads on a National Geographic television show, you have an idea how strongly Paul and Barnabas felt. Sometimes, there's just no give to a situation. You have to stand your ground. Here were two godly men. Two close friends. They had preached together and suffered together. They would do anything for

each other. They would even die for each other. But when it came to John Mark, neither could   or would—budge.

Yet God used their disagreement to double the evangelistic efforts of the early church. Paul went one way and Barnabas went the other. And more churches were established and more people responded to their preaching than had they remained together. Paul and Barnabas weren't the first two godly men to go separate ways, and they certainly weren't the last. Still, I think it's fair to say that they remained friends except for this issue. They loved each other and respected each other—they just couldn't work together.

Eventually, Paul changed his mind about John Mark (1 Tim. 4:11). In fact when Paul was a prisoner in a Roman dungeon, he asked Timothy to be sure and bring Mark when he came.

Are you locking horns with someone you love and respect? Let me encourage you to do everything you can to work it out. *Everything.* And make sure you're not repeating a pattern of behavior. Then, if you must take different paths, take them. But pray for that friend and don't let bitterness take hold. Ask God to bring the friendship full circle in time.

If you're teachable, that's more than likely what will happen.

D r. Paul Stevens, director of the Southern Baptist Radio and Television Commission, served as a chaplain during World War II, stationed in the European theatre. He was on duty at an Army Air Corps base one day when a soldier burst into his office and said there was an emergency in the control tower.

When Stevens arrived, he was told that a shot-up B-17 was circling the airfield but couldn't land. The belly turret had been damaged and wouldn't revolve, trapping the gunner underneath the fuselage. Normally this wouldn't be a concern, but on this occasion, the B-17 pilots couldn't lower the landing gear. For twenty minutes, the crew had been circling the airfield, frantically trying to get the landing gear down.

Everyone knew the score. If the plane landed with the wheels retracted, the gunner would be crushed when the bomber belly flopped onto the runway.

The crew radioed the tower and said they had to land *now*—they were flying on fumes. The controller handed the microphone to chaplain Stevens and said, "The gunner has only two minutes left. He's nineteen years old."

Stevens took the microphone and spoke to the boy. "Son, do you understand the trouble you're in?"

"Yes, sir," the young man replied, voice firm.

"Son, are you ready to meet God?"

"Yes, sir, I am. When I was a boy, my mom took me to church, where I learned that Jesus died for my sins."

"Son, I'm going to ask you to close your eyes. Are your eyes closed?"

"Yes, they are."

"Son, when you open your eyes, you'll be looking into the face of Jesus."

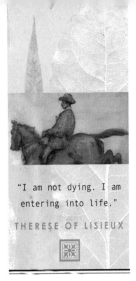

"I am not dying. I am entering into life."

THERESE OF LISIEUX

With that, the chaplain prayed for the gunner. He asked that God would lift him up and welcome him into His arms when the young man arrived in glory. The chaplain was only a sentence or two into his prayer when he heard the horrible sound of the plane hitting the runway.

I don't know how many faith-or-fear issues you face, but I'm certain death is one of them. "It is appointed unto man once to die," Scripture tells us, and what the chaplain said was exactly correct. No matter how God calls us home, Jesus will be waiting to greet us into His presence the instant we draw our last breath.

That's either true or it isn't.

I think it's true.

Now Jabez was more honorable than his brothers, and his mother called his name Jabez, saying, "Because I bore him in pain." And Jabez called on the God of Israel saying, "Oh, that You would bless me indeed, and enlarge my territory, that Your hand would be with me, and that You would keep me from evil, that I may not cause pain!" So God granted him what he requested (1 Chron. 4:9–10).

Let's face it. Most of our prayers are flimsy and routine. We start out with "now I lay me down to sleep" and graduate to "bless this food to our bodies."

Jabez wasn't one for cliches. He didn't pray just because it was expected. He prayed from the gut. When it came to prayer, this guy was bold. He cut very quickly to heart of the matter.

Lord, I want your blessing. Enlarge my territory. Keep me from evil.

It was a simple prayer, but a gutsy prayer.

The most amazing thing to me about the prayer is not the requests but the answer—*God granted him what he requested.* It's one thing to pray for something great. It's another thing to get it.

Jabez got it. God gave him his blessing, enlarged his territory, and kept him from evil.

Here is the question: Why would God answer such a brash prayer?

God answered Jabez in the affirmative because of the character of Jabez. He was *more honorable than his brothers.*

We don't know much about him or his brothers, but we do know this: he was more honorable than they were. And that's why God answered his prayers.

Norman Vincent Peale tells the story, when he was a young boy, of lighting a cigar in the privacy of his bedroom. He had just put out the match when he heard his father coming up the stairs. He blew frantically on the end of the cigar in a futile attempt to put it out. As he heard his father enter the bedroom he quickly hid the cigar behind his back.

When our requests are such as honor God, we may ask as largely as we will. The more daring the request, the more glory accrues to God when the answer comes.

A. W. TOZER

"What was it you wanted to ask me earlier, son?" Norman's father asked.

"Oh, uh, well, I was going to ask if I could go to the lake on Saturday instead of mowing the yard."

His father replied, "Son, never request a favor while hiding a smoldering disobedience."

Too many times we make bold requests of God while hiding a smoldering disobedience. And then we wonder why God doesn't answer in the affirmative.

Jabez was a man of honor. We aren't given any more information than that, but we can assume he was a man of character, integrity, and honesty. To put it another way, Jabez was a righteous man.

No wonder God responded to him.

"The effective, fervent, prayer of a righteous man avails much" (James 5:16). It doesn't say "the effective prayer of a guy holding a smoldering disobedience avails much." When Jabez made his prayer nothing was smoldering.

If it's been awhile since God has responded to your prayers in the affirmative, you might check around for the faint smell of smoke.

t was no ordinary auction. The public was bidding on unclaimed items people had left behind in safe-deposit boxes. Items once deemed so important that people had paid money to safeguard them in steel.

Diplomas, children's report cards, letters . . .

Tables were stacked with coin collections, pocket watches, yellowed documents, and small jewelry items sealed in plastic bags. It was all unclaimed property, waiting to be auctioned—the forgotten or overlooked obsessions of owners now dead.

Two marbles, three stones and a belt buckle . . .

Why these things? Did they represent a special memory, a special person? Why were these marbles so important to somebody?

Rosaries, Boy Scout patches, train tickets . . .

Each bag contained a mystery, the clues doing more to arouse curiosity than to provide answers. The immigration papers of Udolf Matchiner, who arrived at Ellis Island in 1906 were on the table. Did he find what he was looking for in America?

Passports, telegrams, newspaper clippings . . .

An article torn from a 1959 Los Angeles newspaper was headlined, "Vlahovich's Mother Sobs at Guilty Verdict." A mother's son had been convicted of murder. The mother wept, pleading with the judge to spare her son. "Take my blood!" she screamed. "Kill me!" What happened later? Did she watch her son die in San Quentin's electric chair?

Diaries, photographs, the ink print of a newborn's feet . . .

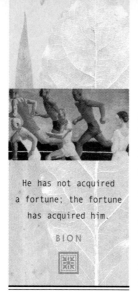

He has not acquired
a fortune; the fortune
has acquired him.

BION

In death's wake, most of the items spoke volumes about life. They also suggested a sense of finality, a poignant reminder that life on earth ends. That everything gets left here.

So what will we leave behind?

A six-by-twelve inch box full of mementos can speak volumes about what we value. But it's only a whisper compared to the legacy of our lives. Amidst our the-one-with-the-most-toys-wins attitudes, perhaps we should dare to leave . . .

> An investment in what God so dearly loves—people.
> A lifelong marriage that defies the odds and demonstrates for the next generation a love that lasts a lifetime.
> An example of a life, guided not by the capricious winds of culture but by the rock-solid promises of Christ.

Ah, heaven—the ultimate safe-deposit box.

The summer Kathleen Kinchline was thirteen, she discovered that rare kind of love found mostly in romance novels. She didn't learn about it from a new boy in town or from a bronzed lifeguard. She learned from a middle-aged father of eight—her dad.

The family was moving from the East Coast to Arizona. Kathleen's mother flew with the baby to Tucson, and the rest of the family piled into the station wagon for the long cross-country drive. After four days of turnpikes and highways, they arrived, tired and grouchy, in Sioux City, Iowa, their mother's hometown.

Everyone was ready for a break. Visiting and playing with their cousins for a couple of days was just what they needed. On the last afternoon of their stay, Kathleen's father took her aside. "Let's go for a ride," he said. "Just you and me." He didn't have to ask twice.

Every landmark absorbed his attention. They drove slowly past the block buildings of downtown Sioux City. They passed the famous stockyards and headed north to the suburb of Leeds. Her father seemed to know where he was going as they wound through the quiet, residential streets.

When they pulled up to a rambling, two-story yellow house her dad switched off the motor. Like all the homes in the neighborhood, this one was set back from the wide tree-lined avenue.

"The house was gray back then," her father said, peering through the windshield.

"Back when?" Kathleen asked.

"A long time ago. That's the house your mother lived in when I first met her," he mused. "I sent a lot of letters to 610 Eighteenth Street."

They stepped out of the car and stood for a moment. *My mother really lived here?* Kathleen wondered to herself.

Her father motioned to her, and they began to walk, each lost in thought. She was still trying to imagine her mother, as a young girl, walking on this same sidewalk.

"Was this street the same when you met Mom?" Kathleen asked.

"Pretty much," replied her father. "Only it was spring when I met her at the USO . . . you know how springtime trees are a bright budding green for a couple of weeks? Well, that's how it was back then—everywhere. I remember lots of tulips and big bushes full of white flowers."

The young girl's curiosity was sparked. "Why were you here, Daddy?"

"I was stationed out at Sergeant Bluff Army-Air Force Base. That's before I joined the paratroopers and went to Europe. I'd take the bus into town and get off back there on Fourth Street. I used to run all the way up to Eighteenth Street. And I never got winded."

They spent a few more minutes gazing at the yellow house. "Your mom and I used to go for a treat a couple of blocks away," said Dad. "If the shop's still there, I'll buy you an ice cream."

Arm in arm they crossed the street to a large

Victorian building facing the intersection. Gallantly, her father stepped in front of Kathleen and opened the arched door. They laughed as he waltzed her into the Green Gables Ice Cream Emporium.

When a marriage works, nothing on earth can take its place.

HELEN DOUGLAS

In a booth by the window, she pondered the delicious dilemma of flavors. "What kind of ice cream did Mom used to get?" she asked.

Her dad thought for a minute. "It was usually chocolate chip."

"Then I'll get chocolate chip, too," she said.

"And I'll order my old favorite: pistachio."

Dad's stories flowed freely while they savored their ice cream. Kathleen listened transfixed, her thirteen year-old imagination recreating every scene. As he spun his tales, his face took on a faraway look.

For the first time in her young life, Kathleen understood that Dad loved Mom in a deep, emotional way. Not only did he love her deeply, but fifteen years of marriage and eight children had not diminished that love at all. Why, he brightened just at the thought of her.

That special afternoon, a father gave his thirteen-year-old daughter a priceless gift: *a glimpse of genuine, romantic married love.* She had no clue anything like this existed until she saw the Real Thing in the clear green eyes of her father.

n a rainy December afternoon, sixteen-year-old Paul Scandrett and his older brother Brad were hiking above the canyon-flanked Skokomish River southwest of Seattle. Paul slipped and fell forty feet into the turbulent, icy water.

They wouldn't find his body until June, fifteen miles downstream.

Paul's death crushed his parents, Greg and Linda. This was not how life was supposed to turn out. A ninety-year-old great-grandfather living in constant pain should die, not a sixteen-year-old boy who has "burp-off" contests with his cousins. A street kid with needle-pocked arms might die of an overdose, not a healthy all-star soccer player who plays the impish shepherd boy in the family's traditional Christmas play.

Greg, a small town Baptist minister, had presided over dozens of funerals and memorial services, but death in his own family taught him things he had never known before.

Death, he learned, is aging ten years in ten days.

Death is a house full of friends and relatives talking in library-soft voices.

Death is a table in the church lobby with childhood photographs and a model airplane and a soccer ball that no one will ever kick again.

A couple of months after Paul's tragic accident, Greg was sitting at the family computer, cleaning out programs and files. When he clicked on several of Paul's programs, the computer asked him, "Are you sure you want to delete?"

Greg wanted to scream, "No! I *don't* want to delete! I don't want his death to be so. . . final!"

And yet it was.

How do parents keep going through such tragedies?

They don't. Many say they feel like they are just existing. The magnitude of pain and suffering for the grieving parents is difficult for anyone to understand. Greg found the mourning process slow and painful. At times, he simply curled up and found a place to cry.

He did find solace when an Arizona pastor, who had also lost a son, shared that his son's death reminded him how trivial some things seemed—like workplace squabbles. And Greg would tell you that he and his wife agree that their priorities are "now in order." They no longer expend energy on small disturbances. Material comforts have no lasting importance.

If your children are alive and well, you have much to be thankful for. Praise God that He entrusted you with their lives, that you can enjoy their infectious laughter, their goofy thinking—even their tendency to blow things out of proportion.

As Psalm 127 reminds us, "Children are a heritage from the LORD; the fruit of the womb is a reward." Enjoy your time with your sons and daughters. Life passes too quickly . . . and we never know what tomorrow may bring.

II heard a story the other day that's a bit aprochryphal, but I like the message.

Jake was growing old and infirm. His memory played tricks on him. He could recall buying his first car, but he couldn't remember what he ate for breakfast.

Day after day, he continued the habit he had begun as a young man: he read his Bible. But he couldn't help noticing that ten seconds after he closed God's Word, he couldn't recall what he had read. His mind was going downhill quickly.

One evening, after going through the same experience, he laid down to rest. Tired, discouraged, and worn out, he told himself it was useless to read the Bible if he couldn't remember what he read from one moment to the next.

He fell into a fitful sleep and experienced a dream as no other. In this dream, he was standing next to a beautiful mountain stream, where crystal-clear water flowed softly over small rocks and boulders. He stood on the river's bank holding a loosely woven basket in one hand.

Suddenly, he saw someone standing on the other bank. He blinked twice, but the sight could not be denied. An angel of the Lord stood in a shining robe.

"I have come to tell you that the Lord your God wants you to fill your basket with living water."

The old man stooped over and dropped his basket into the water. Then he lifted it out and watched all the water drain from the bottom of the basket.

"Don't be discouraged," said the angel. "Try again."

Once more Jake filled the basket with water, but it quickly emptied back into the river.

Disheartened, the old man started to turn away, but the angel called out to him.

"Look into your basket."

Jake dropped his gaze into the basket. What had once been soiled and dirty was now clean and white, sparkling in the sunlight. He marveled at the transformation.

"The Word of God is like the living water that cleaned your basket," the angel said. "Even though you may not recall what you've read recently, you are filling your mind and your heart with God's Word, and it will exert a cleansing, life-giving power in your life."

And then the old man recalled a snatch of Scripture he had once memorized. It was from Psalm 119. David had written, "How can a young man keep his way pure? By living according to your word."

Although he was no longer young, Jake knew God was whispering assurance to his heart through that verse. And the next morning he was up early, reading his Bible. That was something he wasn't going to forget.

> Time spent on the right things is never wasted.
>
> CHARLES R. SWINDOLL

Fred Keissling was a big man, which helps when you're a high school coach. His hands may have been the size of a baseball mitt, but they were the softest hands in Fort Ben Harrison, Indiana, where Fred was the athletic director for the area high school and a golf pro in the summer.

Fred loved teaching youngsters the rudiments of the game. They often came to his junior clinics with little idea of how to play golf—or even how to grip a club. Most of the youngsters used baseball grips instead of interlocking their fingers. Unfortunately, the baseball grips caused youngsters to sway and dip, leading to poor swings and horrible shots.

Whenever Fred saw a poor grip, he stepped behind the youngster, took his own big hands, and wrapped them around the small hands of the youngster. Then he folded the child's hands correctly on the golf club and initiated practice swings, letting the youngster get used to the feel of the new grip.

The new grip usually felt awkward at first, but after several more swings and a few disastrous hits, the most wondrous thing happened: the child began hitting the ball squarely, lofting it high into the distance.

We may not know it, but we are in the Master's grip—a grip that is gentle, loving, and never clenched. He cares enough to reach down and hold our hands in His. What could be more loving, more directional, and more hopeful?

When our life is held in Christ's hands, we can be assured that He has ordained the outcome. You've heard it before but it remains true: *God has a plan for you. A good plan.* The only obstacle to enjoying that plan is running away from it. And that's not a very wise thing to do.

"I know the plans I have for you," God said through the prophet Jeremiah. "Plans to prosper you and not to harm you, plans to give you hope and a future" (Jer 29:11 NIV).

A friend of mine always signs his letters, "In His grip."

That's the safest we can ever be.

In God's grip.

That grip is big enough to hold not only you, but your future as well.

Worried? Anxious? Not sleeping well because of some huge weight?

God's grip is big enough to handle any problem. And He will handle it. It's the least He can do for one of His own.

Life is a voyage that is homeward bound.

BENJAMIN
DISRAELI

e live in an age when words don't mean what they used to, but our language has been subverted for so long that we barely even notice it. What used to be called "killing an unborn baby" is now called "choice." What used to known as "living in sin" is now called a "meaningful relationship." What used to be called "sexual relations" is now called "inappropriate behavior."

How did we get ourselves in this mess? When did we start to turn the meaning of words upside down?

We need to reclaim the true meaning of words because words *do* mean something. *Abstinence* shouldn't be a word that evokes smirks from gum-smacking teenagers. Marital fidelity shouldn't be dismissed as a Victorian-sounding relic—it should be held up as a worthy goal.

Think about it: If politicians can surround themselves with "spin doctors," why can't we surround ourselves with God's Word? I find that continually reading Proverbs is a great way to stay grounded in what words *really* mean. What can be more direct and to the point than listening to what God has to say? Note these examples:

> ➤ Pride, lust, and evil actions are all sins.
> ➤ The wise man saves for the future, but the foolish man spends whatever he gets.
> ➤ A man is known by his actions. An evil man lives an evil life; a godly man lives a godly life.

> God loathes all cheating and dishonesty.

These are direct statements, aren't they? No equivocation, no spin. Anytime you feel the world has polluted the simple meanings of words, turn back to the real Word. We can be confident that when the Bible tells us God is the same yesterday, today, and tomorrow, that means He never changes. We have His word on that.

Truth is heavy, so few men carry it.

JEWISH
PROVERB

God doesn't mince words.
He doesn't play with words.
He doesn't twist words to alter their meaning.
When He says He loves you, He means it.
When He says He has forgiven you, He means it.
God talks straight.
And so should godly men.

Since the day Bobby's dad had died three years ago, the family of five had struggled. Mom worked nights at the hospital, but her small salary could only be stretched so far. Yet what the family lacked in money and material things, they made up for in love and unity.

Bobby, just six years old, had three older sisters who ran the household in their mother's absence. Here it was late afternoon the day before Christmas, and his sisters had each made a beautiful gift for their mother. But he had nothing to give. Wiping a tear from his eye, Bobby kicked the snow and started to walk toward town where the shops and stores were bustling with last-minute shoppers.

Bobby walked from shop to shop, looking into each decorated window. Everything seemed so beautiful —and so out of reach. Suddenly his eyes caught the glimmer of something reflecting along the curb.

He reached down and discovered a shiny dime. Never before had anyone felt so wealthy as Bobby felt at that moment. Clutching the new-found treasure tightly in his hand, he walked into the next store he saw. His excitement quickly turned to despair, however, when salesperson after salesperson told him he couldn't possibly buy anything with just a dime.

Then he saw the flower shop. When the shop owner asked if he could help Bobby, the little boy presented the dime and asked if he could buy at least one little flower for his mother's Christmas gift. The shop owner looked at Bobby and his ten-cent offering.

"You wait here, young man, and I'll see what I can do for you."

Bobby waited as told, looking at the beautiful flowers all around him. Soon the shop owner returned with twelve long-stem red roses, wrapped with leaves of green and baby's breath, all tied together with a big silver bow.

Bobby's heart sank as the owner picked them up and placed them gently into a long white box.

"That will be ten cents, young man," the shop owner said, holding out his hand for the dime. Slowly, Bobby handed the man his dime. Could this be true? Sensing the boy's reluctance, the shop owner explained. "I just happened to have some roses on sale for ten cents a dozen. I hope that will be fine."

The owner held the door as Bobby walked out. He heard the shop keeper say, "Merry Christmas, son," but he didn't notice the man's glistening eyes.

The shop owner's wife, who had been watching the entire transaction, asked, "What was that all about?"

"A strange thing happened to me this morning," he replied. "While I was opening up, I felt impressed to set aside a dozen of my best roses for a special gift for someone. I wasn't sure at the time whether I had

> The promised land always lies on the other side of a wilderness.
>
> HAVECOCK ELLIS

lost my mind or what, but I set them aside anyway. Then just a few minutes ago that little boy came into the shop and wanted to buy a flower for his mother with one small dime. When I looked at him, I saw myself many years ago. I, too, was a poor boy with no money to buy my mother a Christmas gift.

"A bearded man, whom I never knew, stopped me on the street and told me that he wanted to give me ten dollars. When I saw that little boy tonight, I knew where those roses had to go . . . so I put together a dozen of our very best for him."

Just think about that. The shop owner set aside his very best roses for an unworthy boy—and that is what Jesus is doing for us. Although we have nothing to offer Him, not even a dime, He is setting aside a reward for us: eternal life in heaven. All we have to do is walk into His presence and ask humbly for this gift.

Sounds like a pretty good deal to me.

I have a Christian buddy who has little control over his tongue. Given the right situation—the locker room or the basketball court—spicy words roll off of his tongue with the ease of a seasoned sailor.

We go back a few years, so we're comfortable holding each other accountable. When I asked him about his lack of verbal restraint, he just shrugged and looked away. After an awkward moment, he attempted to justify himself.

"Like they say: God redeems the tongue last."

Really now?

I reminded him that Jesus was a carpenter. Carpenters drop things. Sometimes on their big toes. And from time-to-time they swing their hammer without precision, producing a powerful blow to an unsuspecting finger. You've probably witnessed what typically happens next with the average carpenter.

They shout: "#@!*!"

I'm no carpenter, but I've fooled around with wood enough to know that there's some rather dubious discourse lurking behind my *own* lips.

Like when I drop a four-by-four plank on my foot or whack my finger with a hand tool.

Then there's the frustration of cutting a board too short, even after I thought I had measured it correctly . . . twice!

Or the pain of a deeply lodged sliver beneath my uncalloused fingers.

I can think of a fistful of reasons why I might be tempted to speak out of turn.

Personally, I fight it. I desire to control my tongue.

Yet I'm not perfect. Sometimes I blow it.

But I've come to see that taming my tongue is part of my responsibility. So I ask God to give me the strength to reign in this wild beast.

> The tongue is the ambassador of the heart.
>
> JOHN LYLY

The fact that Jesus was a carpenter and never sinned—not even with His words—causes me to marvel. How did He work with wood without losing control of His tongue even *one time?* What about the splinters, smashed fingers, and all? You mean to tell me Jesus never cussed? (Whose name would He have spat out? His own? His Father's?)

No, the Scriptures are clear. Jesus experienced the same type of temptations that you and I encounter.

With one difference.

He never gave in to the Tempter. "For we do not have a High Priest who cannot sympathize with our weaknesses, but was in all points tempted as we are, yet without sin" (Heb. 4:15).

As I shared this perspective of Christ the Carpenter with my friend, all he could do was stare at me, tongue-tied.

Frankly . . . that's not a bad start.

Back in the late '60s, the Ad Council featured a series of anti-smoking commercials aimed at chain-smoking dads. One advertisement pictured a father shooting hoops. His young boy did likewise. When dad washed the car, junior washed his little red wagon. If dad jumped into a pile of freshly raked leaves, his boy did the same.

Cute.

Heartwarming.

But then the twist.

When dad lit a cigarette, the camera zoomed in on the child and asked, "Like father, like son?"

The implication was unmistakable. We learn from what we observe. Therefore, we should set a good example for others.

The Ad Council no longer runs those ads, but we still take our cues from family, from friends, even from key figures in our world.

This matter of imitation is troubling, especially during the late '90s where, as I've noticed, one of the prevailing mantras is: Beat the system. See what you can get away with. Anything goes—just as long as you don't get caught.

Need proof?

Take adultery. We're told it's a private matter between "consenting adults." If you have to lie about it—even under oath—that's understandable. When you're good at what you do professionally, we're told it doesn't matter how you live your life privately.

Or consider tax time. Everyone "fudges" the numbers. Why shouldn't I get "creative" when I report my income and expenses?

And, I must confess, many in ministry speak with forked tongues. When reporting the number of new converts, attendees at a church service, or the response to a mission trip, they speak "evangelaaaaaastically."

Of all commentaries on the Scriptures, good examples are best.

JOHN DONNE

The eighty-five people at last night's service is s-t-r-e-t-c-h-e-d to 123 for the deacons' report.

It's easy in this environment to forget that, in God's eyes, character still matters.

So does integrity . . . virtue . . . and truthfulness.

No wonder the Psalmist prayed for a heart of wisdom (Ps. 90:12). He, just like you and I, desired to be like our Heavenly Father. Not just on the outside—with the "important" things like adultery and murder—but on the inside, in places where the line between right and wrong isn't always clear.

Or in situations where "nobody will ever know." Sure, I'm gonna be tempted to cheat. And the battle over lust will have its challenges. There will be times when I act marginally instead of standing in the gap.

God knew you and I would have such struggles. That's why thousands of years ago He cautioned us with the advice of 1 Corinthians 15:33 "Do not be deceived: 'Evil company corrupts good habits.'" Or, in modern English: Be careful who you hang out with.

Like Father, like son.

How do you do what is right?

It's surprisingly simple. The more time you spend with your Father, the more you'll act like His Son.

hy did you marry your wife? Why didn't you marry another girl? What was it about her that made her special? I would suggest she had some extraordinary traits that made her stand out above all the others. You saw strengths in her that you didn't see in any other woman.

It's almost as though, before you got married, you wore a special set of prescription lenses. And with those lenses, all you could focus on were her strengths. Sure, she had weaknesses, but they were obscure, out-of-focus, and in the background. The strengths of this woman were amazing. They complimented your personality and temperament; together you would be quite a team.

And then came the wedding. You looked good — and she looked unbelievable! As you stood before the pastor, you exchanged vows and placed the ring on her finger. You kissed your bride and turned to the congregation to be introduced as Mr. and Mrs. Then just before you made your way down the steps, your best man reached into his pocket and pulled out a new set of lenses, which you exchanged for your old ones. From here on out, you would focus not on your wife's strengths, but on her weaknesses.

That's why marriage can be heaven or hell. It all depends on where your focus is.

I heard Dr. Howard Hendricks make an astute observation. He said that most people who divorce, divorce over 10 percent of their marriage. If they

Marriage is heaven or hell.

GERMAN
PROVERB

could stand back and look at the big picture, they would see that in the most areas of their marriage, things are okay. But the 10 percent of difficulty becomes so large and blown out of proportion, that the other 90 percent of the relationship is completely ignored.

So where is your focus today? Is it on the 10 percent that drives you crazy or the 90 percent that's in pretty good shape? Have you been focusing exclusively on your wife's weaknesses? No wonder you're frustrated with her. Let me encourage you step to back and look at the big picture. Trade in those lenses that focus on her weaknesses for a pair that will help you to see her strengths.

You married a great woman with both strengths and weaknesses. Give the strengths another chance, and see if it doesn't make a profound difference.

I think Matthew Prior said it best:
Be to her virtues kind,
Be to her faults a little blind.

I had the strangest telephone call the other day. It was from a guy I know who, at the age of forty-two, decided to raise chickens as a hobby. Chickens, of all the crazy things.

"You know, there are more than 200 breeds of chickens these days," he informed me. "I'm raising Rhode Island Reds—they lay those brown eggs."

Okay. But why chickens?

"Did you know that an egg holds within it the highest grade of protein money can buy? Ask any nutritionist. They'll tell you that the protein in an egg runs a close second to mother's milk when it comes to a source for human nutrition."

Um, this is interesting, but I'm kind of busy . . .

"And, Steve, eggs have thirteen key minerals and vitamins plus a perfect blend of amino acids, which are useful for our bodies to build new tissues!"

"See, I've got this writing deadline . . ."

"Frankly, I'm upset about the bad rap egg yolks have received of late. After all, it's the yolk—not the egg white—that has all of these nutrients, plus it has vitamin D. Did you know that egg yolks are one of the few food sources that provide vitamin D?"

"No, but . . ."

"Here's the most interesting part, Steve. Guess what chickens eat?"

I waited.

"Besides their feed, chickens eat bugs. Lot's of them. And they even eat their own droppings!"

Am I missing something here?

Though your sins are like scarlet, they shall be as white as snow; though they are red like crimson, they shall be as wool.

ISAIAH 1:18

"Steve, I'm calling to tell you that the process of making an egg is a lot like salvation! Think about it. A chicken can eat something as foul as droppings and somehow their bodies transform that trash into perfect food."

I'm listening.

"God's in the business of transforming trash into a thing of beauty. And chickens are the perfect example of this process. I can't explain it, but every day they redeem the most unfit food into the most perfect nutrition."

After he hung up, I thought about what he had said.

He was right.

God took me with all of my sinfulness and made me into a new creation. It doesn't matter what trash you or I had ingested in our lives before we came to Christ.

Maybe it was drugs and alcohol.

Perhaps unbridled passion and indiscriminate sex-capades.

Or lying . . . cheating . . . stealing . . . or hatred.

Whatever plagued your past, "though your sins are like scarlet, they shall be as white as snow," (Isa. 1:18).

Through Christ we are cleaned and redeemed.

Hard to believe, isn't it?

If God can transform chicken droppings into perfect protein, He can surely transform me—and all the egg-headed things I've done—into something fit for His kingdom.

So, the next time someone calls you a "chicken" . . . consider it a compliment.

ark Eklund talked incessantly, which drove his third-grade teacher, Sister Anne, to distraction. She had to remind him again and again that talking without permission was not acceptable. What impressed the young teacher so much, though, was his sincere response every time she admonished him for misbehaving.

"Thank you for correcting me, Sister."

Sister Anne didn't know what to make of it at first, but before long she became accustomed to hearing "Thank you for correcting me, Sister" many times a day. One morning, when her patience was growing thin after Mark had talked once too often, she made a novice-teacher's mistake: "If you say one more word, Mark Eklund, I'm going to tape your mouth shut!"

It wasn't ten seconds later when Chuck blurted out, "Sister Anne, Mark is talking again." Since she had stated the punishment in front of the class, she had to act on it.

Sister Anne walked to her desk, deliberately opened a drawer, and took out a roll of masking tape. Without saying a word, she proceeded to Mark's desk, tore off two pieces of tape, and made a big X with them over his mouth. When she glanced at Mark to see how he was doing, he winked at her. That did it! She burst out laughing, and the class cheered as she removed the tape. His first words were, "Thank you for correcting me, Sister."

Six years later, Sister Anne happened to be Mark's junior-high math teacher. One Friday, the students seemed to be intent on picking on each other and creating havoc in the classroom. Anne thought of something that might help their attitudes. She asked the class to list all their fellow students on a piece of paper and leave a space between each name.

A good word costs no more than a bad one.

ENGLISH PROVERB

Then she told them to think of the nicest thing they could say about each of their classmates and write it down beside the appropriate name. That Saturday, on a separate sheet of paper, Sister Anne wrote down the name of each student and listed what everyone else had said about that individual. On Monday she gave each student his or her list. Before long, the entire class was smiling. The exercise had accomplished its purpose: The students were happy with themselves and with each other.

Another six years later, a lightning bolt hit Sister Anne. Her father told her that Mark Eklund, who had been drafted into the Vietnam war, had been killed in action. "The funeral is tomorrow, and his parents would like for you to attend."

After the difficult memorial service, Mark's mother and father approached Sister Anne. "We want to show you something," his father said, taking a wallet out of his pocket.

"They found this on Mark when he was killed. We thought you might recognize it.'

Opening the billfold, he carefully removed two worn pieces of notebook paper that had obviously been taped, folded, and refolded many times. She knew without looking that the papers were the ones on which she had listed all the good things each of Mark's classmates had said about him.

"Thank you so much for doing that," Mark's mother said. "As you can see, Mark treasured it."

Sister Anne couldn't hold back her tears any longer. She cried for Mark and for all his friends who would never see him again. She cried because she saw how God can use the smallest things to lift and encourage people.

What we communicate with our family and the people God puts in our path stays with them in ways we can never imagine.

Have you encouraged anyone today?

o it was, when the people set out from their camp to cross over the Jordan . . . and the feet of the priests who bore the ark dipped in the edge of the water . . . that the waters which came down from upstream stood still, and rose upon in a heap very far away . . . and all Israel crossed over on dry ground (Josh. 3:14–17).

It was a great day for God's people. They had waited for forty years and, finally, it had arrived— they were going to cross over the river Jordan to their new homeland.

They knew it was the right time to cross because God had said so. For three days they had prepared and now they were ready.

But wait a minute! How were they going to cross over? The river was high—in fact, it was the highest it ever got during the year. It was so high, it was overflowing its banks. And there was no bridge.

What were they going to do?

They could have stayed on the riverbank and waited for God to do something. But God had already told them, "Go! Now!"

So they stepped into the water—the priests first and then the people.

Stepping into the water took courage because they didn't know what God was going to do next. They didn't know if God was going to do anything at all. Maybe they would end up with squishy shoes, or worse, be hit by a piece of floating debris or swept away by a strong current. With the river at flood stage, anything was possible.

Stepping into the water was a step of faith. It was a step of obedience.

God couldn't bless them until they did what He had told them to do. And when they obeyed, a miracle happened. God piled all the water of the river into one place. He made a wide path in the riverbed for them to use. And everyone crossed over safely.

Plunge boldly into the thick of life!

JOHANN WOLFGANG VON GOETHE

Is God calling you to step into uncharted waters? How does your faith compare to that of the Israelites at the Jordan? Are you ready to obey Him?

Every new step is just as scary as the first one. If it's not scary, if it doesn't require every ounce of courage and obedience we have, then it's not a true step of faith.

Is God calling you to take a step of faith right now? My faith has been stretched more in the last year than in the previous forty-eight years combined. Twelve months ago I was absolutely terrified of taking a step that my wife and some good friends were encouraging me to take. And as I sit here at this computer today, I'm literally enjoying the blessing of what God called me to do. I'm glad I plunged ahead. To be honest, I really didn't plunge. I was pushed and pulled—not by my wife or friends but by God. I'm glad I didn't resist. And sometimes that's the best you can do.

You may not be sure if God wants you to take the step. And you can tell Him that. But if it's the step He wants you to take, ask Him to push you and pull you. Then give Him your word that you won't resist.

You may be surprised where you are twelve months from now . . . and loving every minute of it!

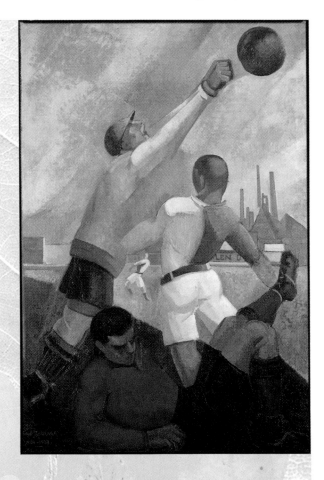

ometimes we men are so results-driven we forget that relationships don't necessarily work that way. If at all.

Case in point. One day a successful businessman took his twelve-year-old son fishing. The night before, they organized all the fishing poles and tackle. Then they put the boat on the car and carefully secured it. They also went out the night before and bought the bait.

Early the next morning they set out for the lake. They rowed to what seemed like a good spot and fished . . . for hours. They tried first this place, then another . . . but to no avail. Not a nibble. Not a bite. They didn't catch a single fish.

At the end of the day they packed up their gear and drove home mostly in silence. It seemed like a wasted day.

Later that night, while preparing for bed, the father mentioned to his wife what a waste of time he thought the whole venture had been.

"I don't think so," she countered. "I have something I think will change your mind."

She went into the other room and returned with the son's diary. She said that while helping him do his homework, he had shown her what he had written for that day's entry: *"Best day of my life. Dad and I went fishing."*

As fathers, sometimes it's just our presence that counts to our children. That's the "results" to them.

We won't have the opportunity to be with them forever. The time will come soon enough when they

One father is more than a hundred schoolmasters.

GEORGE HERBERT

are no longer children, when they are gone.

Perhaps you've heard the old cliché? How do you spell *love*? Answer: T-I-M-E.

How many times do we have to be reminded that at the end of our lives, we won't regret not having accomplished one more professional goal. We won't regret not having made that XYZ sale. We'll regret not having spent more time with our wives and our children.

One family counselor I know says that the only way to ensure his children are on his busy calendar is by putting them on his busy calendar! You can open up his organizer and see their names right there along with his other appointments. This little practice has helped him keep his children a true priority in his life.

The Bible tells us that as fathers we are to rear our children in the fear and admonition of the Lord. But we can't do that very well when we're constantly out of the house and away from them.

How about you? Does your child need your undivided time and attention? Ask God to help you make your family the priority He wants it to be.

Who knows? You may yet treat your child to the best day of his or her life!

And maybe even yours.

e live in "the golden age of excuses." Chuck Colson once remarked that we live at a time where a young man can murder his parents and then beg for mercy in the courtroom because he's an orphan!

We've been called "a nation of victims." People may make all matter of mistakes, but it's not their fault. It's their parents' fault or their kindergarten teacher's fault. No one is responsible for personal actions anymore.

This theme resounds in the feeble excuses people make. Like the flimsy excuses reckless motorists use to explain away their accidents. These are reported to be actual excuses offered up:

- "Coming home I drove into the wrong house and collided with a tree I don't have."
- "I pulled away from the side of the road, glanced at my mother-in-law, and headed over the embankment."
- "I was on my way to the doctor's with rear end trouble when my universal joint gave way, causing me to have an accident."
- "As I approached the intersection, a stop sign suddenly appeared in a place where no stop sign had ever appeared before. I was unable to stop in time to avoid the accident."
- "To avoid hitting the bumper of the car in front, I struck the pedestrian."

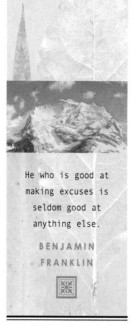

He who is good at making excuses is seldom good at anything else.

BENJAMIN FRANKLIN

As ridiculous as these may seem, is there anything new under the sun? Consider the excuses offered up by our first parents.

After Adam and Eve sinned, they blamed everybody but themselves. Adam blamed Eve, and he even blamed God! He said, "The woman whom you gave to be with me, she gave me of the tree, and I ate" (Gen. 3:12).

And what did Eve do? Take responsibility? No way. She blamed it on the devil. "The serpent deceived me, and I ate" (v. 13).

But you know, we'll never grow up spiritually until we accept responsibility. Paul said, "When I was a child, I spoke as a child, I understood as a child, I thought as a child: but when I became a man, I put away childish things" (1 Cor. 13:11). Included among those childish things should be excuses for misbehavior.

Everybody leaves a trail behind them. In the Old West, a good tracker could learn a lot about a man just by reading his signs.

The trail of a responsible, mature man is easily recognized. There's no sign of an excuse anywhere.

t's been said about the nineteenth-century minister Phillips Brooks, (perhaps best known for his Christmas Carol, "O Little Town of Bethlehem"), that you couldn't know the extent of his kindness until you had done him wrong!

What kind of person can be good and genuinely kind to people who harm him? Only a person ruled by Jesus Christ.

But the way of the world has always been an eye for an eye and a tooth for a tooth. Or its modern-day counterpart: Go ahead. Make my day! That is, do something stupid for which I will blow you away.

D. James Kennedy of Coral Ridge Presbyterian Church likes to tell a story that shows how returning good for evil is superior to returning evil for evil.

Once there was a young wife cooped up every day in a cabin in the snowy mountains of Canada. Her father-in-law, who lived with her and her husband, was a foul-mouthed grouch. He complained about everything, letting forth a string of profanities— knowing this was particularly offensive to her. He was always complaining about something, and the worst part of it was that the harder she tried to please him, the worse he seemed to get. She was trying to maintain a Christian witness in the most trying of circumstances.

So she went to seek the advice of her pastor. He counseled her that the next time her father-in-law acted surly, she should do something kind for him. The minister asked her what the old man liked.

Love your enemies, bless those who curse you, do good to those who hate you, and pray for those who spitefully use you, and persecute you.

MATTHEW 5:43–44Y

"Fudge," she replied. "Especially the way I make it."

This gave the pastor an idea.

"Then the next time he loses his temper, make him some fudge."

It wasn't long before she had an opportunity to try the pastor's advice. She was in the kitchen washing the floor when the grouch stomped in with his dirty boots and complained loudly about the floor being wet. He sat down by the wood-burning stove, dropped his boots on the floor, and rested his smelly feet near the fire. Then he promptly fell asleep.

The young wife got busy. She had all the ingredients on hand to make his favorite treat.

When he woke up, it was to the smell of fudge. He saw a generous plate of it right beside him, together with a mug of fresh coffee.

Tears welled up in his eyes and dripped down onto the fudge. The old hands holding the plate were shaking as he quietly said, "Daughter,

can you come here and forgive a mean, old man?"

When we fight evil with evil, it always increases. It is only when we fight evil with good that the human heart becomes softened.

This is one of the hardest parts of Christianity— to give back good for evil.

To pray for our enemies.

To do good things to those who hate us.

To return good for evil.

But try it next time.

Quite frankly, it's the only alternative that makes any sense.

His nineteen-year-old daughter was beginning her second year at a prestigious college in New England. On a whim, he decided to call the school administration and ask to speak to the person in charge of the spiritual nourishment of the students. The administrator didn't know how to answer. She said no one had ever asked *that* question before.

Then the father recalled a dinner conversation a few weeks earlier. He and his daughter were seated in one of their favorite restaurants, and after a pleasant dinner and jovial conversation, he gently asked her, "What do you believe about God?"

"Well, Dad," she replied, "I believe all that you and Mom have talked about." That's all Beth Ann would say—or could say. The father left the restaurant feeling like he had blown it.

Had he?

Perhaps he had, which is every parent's greatest fear. What can be more important than passing our faith on to those we brought into this world? To those we love the most? Like it or not, our homes are a stage. Our lives are an open book. Our strengths and foibles may be hidden from the world, but they won't stay hidden behind closed doors.

It's the little things that count over the long haul. Praying before meals. Praying as a family during times of crisis. Thanking God for His blessings.

Let your children walk into your bedroom and see you on your knees. Let them hear normal, everyday conversations about your walk with God. Realize that you—the father and God-ordained spiritual leader in the home—set the spiritual thermostat around the house.

Set it too high, and kids rebel. Set it too low, and kids never warm up to the Lord. Maybe Beth Ann wasn't ready to talk about her faith that night with her father . . . or maybe the thermostat had been set too low in their home.

> Believe on the Lord Jesus Christ, and you will be saved, you and your household.
>
> ACTS 16:31

Whatever spiritual temperature we set in our homes, we can't *force* our children into decisions for Christ, nor can we *make* them believe what we believe. But that's what keeps us on our knees—and checking up on that thermostat.

Remember the singing comedian of the 1960's, Allen Sherman, who's camp song "Hello Muddah, Hello Fadduh" hit the top of the charts?

It took him a long time to make it to the top. After achieving fame and fortune, he was asked to write an article about how he became "an overnight success." So he wrote the article and entitled it: "How I Became an Overnight Success in Eighteen Years!"

And so it goes. The same principle of hard-earned success applies to all of life. Rarely does true success come easily.

A successful pianist once remarked that if he didn't practice his set number of hours every day (I think it was ten!), he would notice the difference. But if he went two days in a row without practice, the audience would notice the difference.

However, too often in our instant culture with instant this and instant that, we think success comes instantly too: Just add water, put it in the microwave, and voilà!

But success generally doesn't work that way. It takes time and dedication. It means plodding along when you'd rather be at the beach.

Think about Noah building the ark. Day after day, he labored. He had never seen one drop of rain much less a flood. But he believed God, and he kept on doing all the hard work the God had commanded. It took Noah 120 years to build that boat, but by the grace of God, he and his whole family were saved because of their persistence and hard work.

So we must persist if we want to be successful. Even spiritual success doesn't come overnight. Through patience and perseverance, God builds our character. Virtually nothing of lasting value comes easy.

Ironically, the opposite is not true. The results of a successful life can be torn down completely in a five-minute rage or a half-hour affair. Think of a building that can be torn down in less than an hour. It may have taken many months, perhaps years, of diligent labor to lay the foundation and construct the rest of the building. Yet the whole thing can be dynamited and destroyed within minutes!

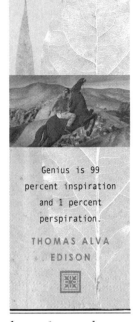

Genius is 99 percent inspiration and 1 percent perspiration.

THOMAS ALVA EDISON

Hard work can be overturned overnight, but it can't be accomplished overnight.

So keep plodding.

Keep showing up.

Keep being faithful

And at the right time, when your character has grown sufficiently to handle it, God will grant you success.

And because you took the long road to get there, you'll be very careful of any foolish move that might take it from you.

hen it comes to restaurants, most guys think of one thing: food. But certain restaurants do more than sell food. They provide *atmosphere*. Or to put it another way, *ambiance*. I looked that word up: It means *expensive*.

In every town there is at least one dive in the run-down side of town where you have to reserve a table. The upholstery is torn and the Formica tables are stained, but customers are waiting to get in. Why? Because of the quality of the food. And most of the people waiting to get in are men—men who don't give a rip about atmosphere.

Every once in a while, on a special occasion, I'll take my wife out to a restaurant that has not only good food, but great atmosphere. And I've noticed a correlation: The nicer the atmosphere, the higher the check. But on your wedding anniversary, you're going for the greatest atmosphere possible. Right?

Where is all this talk about atmosphere heading? Think back to when you were ten years old. Think back to where you lived. Where you went to school. Who your friends were. Who your teacher was.

When you were ten, what was your family like? Do you look back with fond memories or with pain? What kind of marriage did your folks have? Or were they divorced? What kind of relationship did you have with your dad?

To put it another way, when you were ten years old, what was the atmosphere of your home?

As restaurants have atmospheres, so do homes. And I'm convinced that the husband/father sets the atmosphere in each home. Even if he's absent, he has set the atmosphere.

Let the wife make her husband glad to come home and let him make her sorry to see him leave.

MARTIN LUTHER

Generally speaking, the atmosphere in each home is one of two kinds: constructive or destructive. In a constructive atmosphere, wives and children are built up. In a destructive atmosphere, wives and children are torn down.

When you were ten, what the atmosphere of your home? Was your mother built up, or was she torn down? How about you? Were you built up by your father, or did he tear you down?

There's not much any of us can do about the home we were raised in. But there's plenty we can do about the homes we live in. You're the man of the house—you set the atmosphere.

So how about it? Do you build your wife up? Or have you slipped into the habit of tearing her down? If you build her up, your kids will be built up. If you tear her down, you'll do the same to your kids. Even if you don't intend to.

Atmosphere affects everyone.

And only you can change it.

Do you ever feel overwhelmed by evil? Just open the newspaper or turn on the evening news, and it bombards you. All the brutality and the cruelty of man astonishes me. Nowadays we hear about what would have been unthinkable twenty years ago.

Kids killing kids.

People beaten and killed for next to nothing.

People hurting others simply for the "fun" of it.

One of the worst events I ever heard about was when some teenagers fatally shot an ice-cream truck driver. Then, as he writhed in pain on the ground, they danced around him in celebration and helped themselves to the goodies in his truck.

It is awful and terrifying, this capability for evil.

We see corruption in the courts, where some gain great wealth by taking advantage of those who can't defend themselves. Justice seems to be a matter of money. As someone quipped, "We have the best justice money can buy!"

Evil is all around us, but horror of horrors . . .

Evil is *within* us.

Remember the classic story of how a Jewish Holocaust survivor group caught one of the most evil war-criminals? One of them doggedly attended the trial of the ex-Nazi, only to lament: "He's just like me!" An ordinary man, guilty of extraordinary evil.

Evil is within us. It's within you. It's within me.

Have you ever had the experience of being high up somewhere holding a baby? Maybe you're on a balcony or the top of a building and suddenly an

unbelievable thought comes into your brain:
Jump.

Or worse . . . *Toss the baby down!*

Where do such thoughts come from? I believe it's entirely possible that they're whispered into our ear by the evil one.

It's one thing to know that the times are evil. It's another thing to acknowledge the abyss in our own hearts. Paul talks about this in his letter to the Romans: *Evil is within me, and that which I don't want to do, I do.*

So how do we overcome evil? Or at least keep it in check?

Much of the answer is determined by what we feed our souls. Good input, good output. Bad input, bad output.

That may seem simplistic, but it's true.

It's like the classic story Bill Bright of Campus Crusade used to tell about the Indian who had two dogs—one white and one black—that he would have fight each other. One day somebody asked him how he knew in advance which one would win. He answered, "Oh, that's easy. The one I feed is the one that'll win!"

And so it is with us.

If we feed the sin nature—with pornography, drug use, or suggestive television-viewing— the output will be predictable.

During these wicked days, don't let evil gain even a toehold in your life.

Starve the bad dog . . . and feed the good one.

It is right noble
to fight wickedness
and wrong; the mistake
is in supposing that
spiritual evil can
be overcome by
physical means.

LYDIA CHILD

ecently, I spent three days alone in my home while the rest of the family visited relatives.

Though I wanted to go with them, I chose to stay behind and play catch-up with work deadlines that needed my undivided (not to mention undistracted) attention. I watched my family drive away, waved good-bye, and turned back to the silent house.

Three days alone. No kids. No schedule. No demands on my time or my plans. I could eat when I was hungry, not when dinner was ready. I could work through bedtime and beyond and not lose my stride by having to get up and tuck anyone in bed or get someone a glass of water.

No need to stop what I was doing and answer a question, listen to a complaint, or break up an argument. No one else's music, television, or problems would distract me. I was alone. All alone. For three whole days.

Time . . . silence . . . solitude. A rare, rich treat. A luxury.

But I couldn't stand such a luxury all the time. It would be like living on a steady diet of truffles. Or cheese cake. Or caviar. They're all enjoyable in small doses, but imagine eating food like that all the time! Not only would you get tired of such a diet, you'd also get fat, lazy, and self-indulgent.

The one time I ate caviar was at a moderately upscale seaside restaurant where it was being served alongside other appetizers at a salad bar. It wasn't the priciest caviar, no doubt, but caviar nonetheless. I scooped some onto a cracker or two and returned to my table, relishing not only the rich saltiness of the delicacy but the accompanying air of elegance. It was great for a rare treat, but not for a steady diet.

No man can safely mingle among people save he who would gladly be solitary, if he could.

THOMAS A'KEMPIS

The same is true of solitude It's good in small doses. But not as a steady diet. The effort required to think of others— giving your time, your space, your attention—keeps you spiritually healthy. It forces you to look outward. And that's good for you. Good for your soul.

Caviar moments in life should be a rare treat. The common, everyday fare—tucking kids into bed, answering questions, putting down your pen, getting a glass of water—this is the staff of life.

The bread . . . the meat . . . that keeps the soul healthy.

It's a quiet, sunny Saturday morning—perfect for waxing the car.

First, I do the basic wash, to remove any bugs and loose dirt. Then comes the more demanding work. Trying to remove road tar smudges behind the wheel walls—black streaks and blotches of oily goo.

Every time I wax the car I tell myself I'm going to spend some extra time rubbing away those grimy stains. But that kind of rubbing takes time. And it's not as early as it was when I first started. Besides, I buy the kind of wax that goes on fast and wipes off shiny—the no-muss-no-fuss-quick-and-easy kind. I can be done with this job in no time.

What to do, then, about those road-tar smudges? What I usually do on a Saturday that's rapidly passing me by. I take my quick-and-easy car wax and polish right over those smudges, trying not to look too closely. I convince myself that I'll get around to removing them someday when I have more time. Pretty soon I have a clean, shiny car, with glossy tar smudges glistening behind the wheel wells.

Road tar entombed in car wax?

Shiny smudges?

This looks familiar.

Looks a little like me.

Jesus had something to say about layers of dirt entombed beneath a sheen of polish. *"Woe to you, teachers of the law and Pharisees, you hypocrites! You are like whitewashed tombs, which look beautiful on the outside but on the inside are full of dead men's bones and everything unclean! In the same way, on the outside you appear to people as righteous but on the inside you are full of hypocrisy and wickedness"* (Matt. 23:27–28, NIV).

A scab is a scab, even if you smear honey on it.

JEWISH PROVERB

Is my soul like a white-washed tomb—beautiful on the outside, but underneath, full of dirt? A casual observer might notice how faithfully I attend Bible studies, mentor other believers, put away chairs after church, and be impressed. What a good Christian!

But what if he peered closer? What if he took a rag and rubbed away the outer layer of polish? What would he see? A short temper? A covetous heart? An envious spirit? An impatient demeanor? *Smudges?*

It's not enough to sweep over the surface of our souls, to push the dirt around with a rag or a sponge and cover it up with polish. A well-cleaned soul must be stripped of all pretense. What does it take to examine your soul? It takes getting down on your hands and knees before God, admitting to Him all that you are: ill-tempered, covetous, envious, impatient. It also takes admitting to others that you're not as flawless as they think, and asking them to pray for you. It takes the scouring cleanser of honesty and humility before God and others to purge our souls of hypocrisy.

It's never
too late to apply
the rigorous
cleansing of
reality and
repentance to
a neglected soul,
and become—
inside and out —
thoroughly clean.

t was a gorgeous February afternoon in Florida. Sunlight reflected against the water of the Miami River where seventeen-year-old Nancy Burns sat inside a 1969 Mach I Mustang, gazing out at the marina. The car was parked on the marina lawn, about two feet from the edge of the seawall. Outside the car, Nancy's boyfriend, Mark Smith, who washed cars on weekends to earn extra money, washed and polished the car while Nancy waited inside.

Sitting in the passenger seat, Nancy began to grow restless. She reached over to the driver's seat and turned the key, which was still in the ignition. Intending to turn the key only one notch, Nancy mistakenly started the car. It lurched forward toward the seawall and plummeted over the edge into the marina. There was no time for her to escape.

Thus began the longest fifteen minutes of her life. While Mark's father called for emergency rescue, Mark dove again and again, trying unsuccessfully to locate the car in the murky depths. By the time rescuers arrived, five minutes had passed, and no one believed Nancy could still be alive.

She was. Keeping her cool, she managed to locate a pocket of air near a window. While divers frantically attempted to free her, she pressed her face against the shrinking air bubble. Nearly fifteen minutes went by before she finally passed out. But by then, firefighter Larry Norton, on the last second of air himself, managed to pry open the passenger door, locate Nancy, and drag her to the surface.

One minute more and both Nancy and Larry would have perished.

Minutes. How many of us, during the course of our day, bother to consider the value of a minute? In a matter of minutes, cities have been demolished by earthquakes, homes destroyed by fire, and lives snuffed out by the random gunfire of gang violence. It took less than a minute for an atomic bomb to destroy nearly five square miles of Hiroshima and hundreds of thousands of lives. One minute Joni Eareckson Tada was a vibrant, healthy teenager, about to dive into a lake. The next, she was floundering beneath the surface, near death, her neck broken, completely paralyzed.

What is your life? You are a mist that appears for a little while and then vanishes"

JAMES 4:14 NIV

Minutes. Every minute somebody dies. Somebody's life is changed, perhaps scarred forever. A matter of minutes—that's all it takes for all that we've worked for and all that we've dreamed about to come to nothing.

We can go along our entire lives thinking we're okay, we're doing fine. But the moment will come when we'll have to face the truth the wealthy landowner in Luke's gospel faced: "This night your soul will be required of you" (Luke 12:20). We'll pass from this world into the presence of God. In that instant, our place in eternity will be clear. We'll either be held accountable for our sins and judged accordingly, our we'll be welcomed into God's presence, completely forgiven.

Minutes. That's all it takes for our eternal destiny to be decided. A word spoken, a prayer of repentance —the choice is ours. We can be set free from the power of sin and death in our life and be at peace with God.

All in a matter of minutes.

*The true story of Nancy Burns was adapted from *Minutes to Live*, by Judith Stone (Raintree Publishers, 1980).

t was late. We were driving home from a visit to the desert and took a short cut through the mountains. We had hoped the children would sleep the entire way, but no such luck. For some reason, the baby was inconsolable. We tried everything—the pacifier, quiet lullabies, gentle strokes, a bottle—nothing worked.

There we were, in the middle of the night on a winding mountain road with a screaming baby in the back seat. What to do? In a moment of weakness— and against our better judgment—we yielded to what we knew she wanted. My wife reached around to the back seat, unstrapped the car seat, and lifted the baby into her arms. Within minutes, the baby was quiet. She rested her head against my wife's shoulder and fell fast asleep.

What did that little baby want? Not food, not meaningless songs or empty words. Strapped in a cold, hard car seat in the dark, she wanted one thing only: the security of her mother's arms.

Little did she know, however, how *insecure* she really was. Headlights approaching in the night are unpredictable. Would they suddenly veer into us? Would we miss that next curve and go over the edge? My wife's arms would be useless to save her in such a case. The baby's sense of security was, in fact, an illusion. In reality, she was much safer screaming in her car seat than she was sleeping soundly in her mother's arms.

If your security
is based on something
that can be taken
away from you, you
will constantly be
on the false edge
of security.

TIM HANSEL

We all have our ideas about what constitutes security. There's financial security: money in the bank, a good retirement plan. There's emotional security: a strong marriage, contented children. There's physical security: locks on the door, neighborhood watch.

Then there's spiritual security. Some people feel spiritually secure living a good life or attending church regularly. Some live a carefree life uncomplicated by thoughts of religion, while others are secure believing there's no God other than themselves.

All of these ideas of security—financial, emotional, physical, spiritual—appear trustworthy. They offer solace. So we reach out for them, just like my little baby found solace in her mother's arms. But that baby, lulled to sleep by the warmth of familiar arms, didn't know how perilously close to disaster she really was. And even though you and I may feel comfortable with our own perception of security, we, too, are in danger of being lulled to sleep, resting in the arms of an illusion.

Is it enough to go through life content with our own perception of security, unaware how dangerously close to the edge of the cliff we really are? The Bible

speaks uncompromisingly of coming judgment. The truth is, none of us will escape it. And when that day arrives, our money, our relationships, the locks on our doors, even our personal perception of who God is will be useless.

The only "arms of safety" from God's judgment are the arms of His Son, Jesus Christ. God has provided us with an opportunity to be secure, not just in this life but for eternity. He reaches out to us with arms of compassion and mercy.

This is the security of reality.

It sure beats the uncertainty of illusion.

oney is a tough subject. It's hard to get a grip on. Vic Oliver put it this way:

> If a man runs after money, he's money-mad; if he keeps it, he's a capitalist; if he spends it, he's a playboy; if he doesn't try to get it, he lacks ambition. If he gets it without working for it, he's a parasite; and if he accumulates it after a lifetime of hard work, people call him a fool who never got anything out of life.

The Bible has quite a bit to say about money. Money can be a snare, a trap that can ruin your life. On the other hand, you have to have it to take care of your family.

What's the single most important financial principle? I'm sure everyone has an opinion on that, but let me give you mine.

First, let me say that I'm making some assumptions here. I'm assuming that a man is following Christ with his whole heart. I'm assuming that man loves Christ instead of money. I'm also assuming that his motive is to please God in everything he does. Given those assumptions, I think the most important financial principle in the world is this: *Give, and it will be given to you.*

Think about it for a minute. A lot of guys are working hard enough to get a stroke simply to leverage their money. They're looking for a return on their investment—an absolutely sure thing.

"Give, and it will be given to you."

Now that's a sure thing. It's not backed by the FDIC—it's backed by your heavenly Father. If you give, God will give to you. Guaranteed.

Now let's consider the reverse of that principle.

"Don't give, and it won't be given to you."

That's not as appealing, is it? And why would a man *not* give? Because he thinks he can't afford to give. But therein lies *trust*. It's where faith in the promise of God comes in.

If you make money your god, it will plague you like the devil.

HENRY FIELDING

The context of that promise goes like this: "Give, and it will be given to you: good measure, pressed down, shaken together, and running over will be put into your bosom. For with the same measure that you use, it will be measured back to you" (Luke 6:38).

It's the potato chip principle . . . but I'm out of space. So if you're interested in a few more chips, let's move on to the next chapter.

'll level with you.
I'm not into prosperity theology.
But that doesn't keep me from potato chip theology.

The concept is found in Luke 6:38: "Give, and it will be given to you: good measure, pressed down, shaken together, and running over will be put into your bosom. For with the same measure that you use, it will be measured back to you" (Luke 6:38).

Think back to the last time you bought a bag of potato chips. Disappointing, wasn't it? The bag was only half full. When they filled it the bag was full, but in transit the chips settled.

God says, "When you give, I'll give back to you." When He fills a bag of chips, He shakes it down so He can put as many chips as possible into that bag. In fact, He puts so many chips in the bag, you can't close it.

God doesn't want his people disappointed.

No half-full bags from Him.

It's all you can do to keep them from spilling out.

Did you notice that the measure of your giving is the measure He uses to give back to you? If you give with a teaspoon, He'll give back to you using the same teaspoon. If you use a gallon jug, He'll use a gallon jug. If you use a dump truck to measure out your giving . . . well, you'd better add some storage space.

So what's our problem with giving? Why is it so hard?

Giving is hard because our nature is to *accumulate*. America is a nation of accumulators. We're after as much as we can get. And when you're trying to accumulate, giving gets in the way.

Remember what Jesus said? "Where your treasure is, there your heart will be also" (Matt. 6:21).

Let's cut to the chase. You can either trust in money or you can trust in God. If you trust in God, you're freed up to give money away. If you don't trust in God, there's no way you're going to give.

Let us give according to our incomes, lest God make our incomes match our gifts.

PETER MARSHALL

The giver knows that God provided the money in the first place. That money isn't his—it's God's.

Jesus made it very clear in Matthew six that God has promised to meet every one of our needs. We don't need to be anxious. Three times He said that. We don't need to be anxious because our Father knows what we need. If He takes care of the birds, He'll certainly take care of us.

Does the Bible say "Seek *third* the kingdom of God"? I don't think so.

Jesus said, "Seek *first* the kingdom of God and His righteousness, and all these things shall be added to you" (Matt. 6:33).

If God is first in your life, you can give.

If He's first in your life, He'll give you more.

Why? Because money doesn't have your heart— He has your heart.

And that's what He's been after all along.

oshua did as Moses said to him and fought with Amalek. And Moses and Aaron and Hur went up to the top of the hill. And it was when Moses held up his hand, that Israel prevailed; and when he let down his hand, Amalek prevailed. But Moses' hands became heavy, so they took a stone and put it under him, and he sat on it. And Aaron and Hur supported his hands, one on one side, and the other on the other side. And his hands were steady until the going down of the sun. So Joshua defeated Amalek with the edge of the sword* (Exod. 17:8–13).

Our culture teaches us to do it alone.

It teaches us to strike out on our own and do it our way.

It teaches us self-reliance.

But the Bible teaches that we need each other. We're the body of Christ, and each part needs the other. No man is an island.

Take the battle scene in Exodus. Moses and his people were on their way to the Promised Land when they were viciously attacked by the Amalek gang. The Amalekites were desert dwellers who would attack anyone, but they had a special beef against the Moses crowd. Actually, it was more like a family feud. Their ancestor Esau had been tricked out of his inheritance by his brother, Jacob. As a result, the Amalekites had moved to the desert. But even after hundreds of years, they still carried a grudge against Jacob's descendants. So when they heard Moses was moving into their territory, they decided to attack.

They were vicious and sneaky. They attacked from the rear, picking off stragglers—the ones who were tired and weary (Deut. 25:17).

Moses decided to call a showdown. He appointed Joshua as commander-in-chief of the battle. Moses himself stayed up on a hilltop where everyone could see him as he lifted his hands up in prayer. In his hands he held the rod of God.

True friendship is loyalty to a friend in trouble.

RALPH BREWER

Moses lifted up the rod of God for two reasons. First, he wanted to encourage the people. Every time they looked up, he wanted them to know that God was watching over them and would give them victory. The rod was like a banner; Jehovah-Nissi means "God is my banner." Moses wanted the people to see that they were fighting under the flag of the Lord God Almighty.

Second, Moses lifted up the rod to show that he was praying for the people. Every minute they were fighting, he was praying for their success, for their victory.

But a problem developed. As the battle raged on all day, Moses' hands grew tired. He couldn't hold them up. But whenever he dropped his hands, the Israelites began to lose. They kept winning only as long as he held his hands up.

What was Moses to do? He knew he couldn't do the job alone. So he called on Aaron, his brother, and Hur, his brother-in-law, to help him.

First Aaron got a stone for Moses to sit on so he could stay on the hilltop as long as necessary. Then Aaron got on one side of Moses and propped up one arm, and Hur got on the other side and propped up the other arm.

Do you know the result of this "team" effort? Moses was able to hold up his arms all day, until the

sun went down. Israel won a great victory that day.

Are you worn out from the battle?

Do you feel like you're all by yourself?

Let me give you a tip: Don't let the enemy paint you into a corner of isolation. Tell your wife that you're hurting. Call a friend and tell him what's going on. And ask them to hold up your arms. You'll be surprised how willing they are to help. And it sure beats fighting the battle by yourself.

So what's the moral of this story? *You can't live the Christian life by yourself.* Period. Or as the song says, "We all need somebody to lean on."

That's not only a good song. It's biblical.

n April, 1992, a young man named Chris McCandless hiked into the Alaskan wilderness alone. Four months later, a party of moose hunters found his body in an abandoned bus. He had starved to death.

In trying to piece together the missing parts of the puzzle that would explain how and why McCandless died, author Jon Krakauer wrote a book called *Into the Wild*. Yet Krakauer doesn't write strictly as an impartial journalist. He writes as one who understands the impulses that drive people to such apparent foolhardiness. One who himself, at the age of twenty three, attempted a solo climb of the great northern wall of an Alaskan glacier called Devil's Thumb. The feat had never been accomplished before.

Krakauer proceeds to convey the details of his ultimately unsuccessful attempt to climb the northern wall: the terror of storms that buffeted him while he clung precariously over the abyss beneath him; the growing realization that he didn't want to die alone at the bottom of some crevasse on an Alaskan glacier; the excruciating disappointment of defeat.

It's not only gripping reading but an amazing testimony of grit, audacity and, to a certain degree, *faith*. To inch your way up the vertical slope of a frozen wall, trusting that the placement of your picks, the efficacy of your equipment, and the stability of the ice will keep you from crashing to an icy death, takes an extraordinary amount of faith in something.

Some might call it temerity—and they would probably be correct. But I also call it *faith*. I don't know if Jon Krakauer has faith in God or not, but one thing is sure: he had a sit-up-and-take-notice kind of faith that propelled him halfway up the side of a glacier.

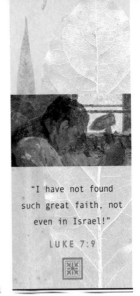

"I have not found such great faith, not even in Israel!"

LUKE 7:9

Imagine having a faith in God that rivals the kind of faith Jon Krakauer had while climbing his wall of ice. An audacious faith. A faith that amazes.

Only once in the Bible (Luke 7:1-10) is Jesus actually amazed by a person's faith—a centurion who had sent some Jewish elders to Jesus, asking Him to come and heal his servant. The elders made sure Jesus understood just who He was dealing with: a VIP of Israel. Whether or not Jesus was impressed isn't clear, but He did accompany the elders back to the centurion's home.

Before He arrived, however, another party intercepted Him with a new message from the centurion. "Lord, do not trouble yourself, for I am not worthy that you should enter under my roof. Therefore I did not even think myself worthy to come to You. But say the word, and my servant will be healed."

These words stopped Jesus in His tracks. This VIP, this luminary of Israel, didn't feel worthy even to appear in Jesus' presence, let alone have Jesus step across the threshold of his home. Instead, he was content for Jesus merely to "say the word." Jesus was amazed. And He said so.

Amazing faith. Peerless faith. Faith that turns heads. Faith so saturated in God's eminence, glory, and majesty that, in spite of his own celebrity and recognition, the centurion felt completely unworthy to be in Christ's presence. At the same time, faith so confident in God's mercy, compassion, and love that, in spite of his acute sense of unworthiness, he was assured he could ask for the thing he desired.

Amazing faith.

A faith that doesn't just climb mountains—it moves them.

arlier, we touched on Noah's hard work in building the ark—120 years of hard work. We saw how perseverance and hard work are crucial to success. Now let's look at Noah a little closer.

Noah lived at a time when the whole world was "going to the dogs." It was so vile and corrupt that there was only one decent family left: Noah, his wife, their three sons, and their son's wives—eight people.

God saw how corrupt the world was and how decent Noah and his family were. God told Noah, "I wish I had never created the world. In 120 years I'm going to destroy everything in it except you and your family and some of the animals. I'm going to drown everything in a worldwide flood. I'm telling you this now because so you will have time to prepare. I want to save you."

God told Noah exactly what to do. He told him to build an ark. It was to be huge: 450 feet long by 75 feet wide by 45 feet high—about the same size as a modern day battleship. But at that time, no one had ever built anything like it. It wouldn't be made to sail, but to float. It wouldn't be steered; it would simply float on the surface of the water. The higher the floodwaters rose, the higher the ark would be lifted up towards heaven.

It would be made of gopher wood, also called cypress. It's a wood noted for its lightness and durability, and was the wood of choice for the best shipbuilders in the world, the Phoenicians.

The ark would have three decks, divided into compartments. It would have one window located eighteen inches from the top and a door on its side. It would be covered inside and out with pitch so it wouldn't leak.

A winner never quits, and a quitter never wins.

ANONYMOUS

Can you imagine the reaction of Noah's neighbors when he started on such a project? They must have laughed themselves silly: "Noah, the nut case, thinks it's going to rain. Noah, preparing for a storm. The only storms we have here are sand storms!"

Noah had never built an ark before, but he worked with unswerving confidence. In spite of the ridicule, he persevered. It was hard to collect all the wood he needed. Hard to cut it and join it together and cover it with pitch. It was a long job. At the same time, he kept warning everyone he saw, trying to tell the people what was going to happen.

What if he had given up? What if, after 100 or 110 years, Noah had said, "I've had it. That's enough. I'm tired of pounding this wood, and I'm tired of the whole world pounding me. Maybe I really didn't hear God."

But perseverance brought preservation.

When Noah finished his task, God told him exactly when the flood would come—in only seven

more days. God told him to get into the ark. God also told Noah how long the rain would last—forty days. Later He showed Noah when it would be safe to get out of the ark. Because Noah persevered, God gave him an exact timetable of events and a promise to keep him safe.

This world is strewn with half-completed projects and people who didn't finish what they started. If you want to be successful in the kingdom of God during your time on earth, then persevere, persevere, persevere!

Or as Winston Churchill put it in one of his most famous speeches, "Never give up! Never, never, never, never give up."

That means you . . . and me.

he violent grinding of brakes and the harsh creaking of skidding wheels died as the big car came to a sudden stop. Young Eddie picked himself up from the dusty pavement where he had been thrown, and looked around wildly.

Susie! Where was his little sister? He had been holding her hand when they started across the street. The next moment, he turned and saw her under the big car that had run them down. Her eyes were closed and a dark stain was spreading slowly across her white sweater.

It seemed like forever before sirens announced the arrival of help. Susie was quickly examined, delicately put on a stretcher, then loaded into the ambulance. Eddie was allowed to ride in the back with her, and he held her hand all the way to the hospital. Something about the shabbily dressed boy, who couldn't be more than twelve years old, and his devotion to his sister touched the hearts of the hardened medical technicians.

"We must operate at once," the surgeon said after a preliminary examination. "She's been injured internally and has lost a great deal of blood."

Eddie waited in the sitting room while the surgeons worked on Susie. After what seemed like an eternity, a nurse came looking for him.

"Eddie," she said kindly, "your sister is hurt very badly. The doctor wants to make a transfusion. Do you know what that is?"

Love is my decision
to make your problem
my problem.

ROBERT SCHULLER

Eddie shook his head. He had never even heard the word before.

"She's lost so much blood that she can't live unless someone gives her blood," the nurse explained. "Will you do that for her?"

Eddie's wan face grew paler, and he gripped the arms of the chair so hard that his knuckles became white. For a moment he hesitated; then gulping back his tears, he nodded his head and stood up.

"You're a fine young man," the nurse said, as she whisked him away to the elevator and the operating room. No one spoke to Eddie except the nurse who quietly directed him how to prepare for the ordeal. The boy bit his quivering lip and silently obeyed.

"Are you ready?" asked a man swathed in white from head to foot, turning from the table over which he had been bending. For the first time Eddie noticed who it was lying there so still. Little Susie! And he was going to make her well.

Two hours later, the surgeon looked up with a weary smile. "I think she's going to pull through," he said.

"That's wonderful news, doctor," exclaimed one of the young interns. "A miracle!" Nothing, he thought, could be greater than the miracles of science.

After the transfusion, Eddie had been told to lie quietly on a cot in the corner of the room. In the excitement of the delicate operation, he had been entirely forgotten. As the doctor turned to explain the good news, he was caught off-guard when Eddie quietly asked, "When do I die?"

"Die? What do you mean, son?" the doctor asked.

"I thought . . . when they took somebody's blood . . . he died," whispered Eddie.

The smiles faded from the lips of the doctor and the nurses. The young intern, who had thought there was nothing greater than the miracle of modern science, caught his breath.

This soft-spoken lad had climbed to the very heights of devotion and sacrifice. He had shown them a glimpse of the greatest miracle of all—selfless love!

The kind of love Jesus demonstrated when He died on the Cross.

He didn't consider His rights

He didn't consider what was best for Himself.

He simply paid the debt we could never pay.

A number of years ago the force of that love cause a man to pen these words: *"Amazing love, how can it be? That Thou, my God, should'st die for me?"*

That's the gospel.

And when you begin to understand it, it will take your breath away.

Mike was moving his family of four from smog-choked Los Angeles to the high, blue skies of Colorado. After the movers loaded the van with all their belongings, the family jumped into their car for the trip east.

About ten o'clock that hot August night, the family turned wearily off Interstate 15 into Las Vegas—city of excess, gateway to garish casinos and overwrought hotels. They had reserved one of those twenty-nine dollar specials at the Excalibur Hotel, an intimate and cozy inn with 4,200 rooms crammed into twenty-seven stories overlooking the neon-lit Strip. Tired, cranky, and out of sorts, the young family dragged their heavy luggage past thousands of slot machines and gaming tables to reach the elevator. They were anxious to sleep.

The next day at checkout time, Mike told his wife, Nicole, that he was making a first trip to the car with a couple of bags. He took along his seven-year-old son, Patrick, to give him something to do. Outside the hotel, the triple-digit heat seared the blacktop as father and son trudged toward the far reaches of the Disneyland-sized parking lot. Then, wouldn't you know it? When they arrived at the car, Mike discovered he had forgotten the keys.

The last thing he wanted to do was lug the heavy bags all the way back to the hotel room on the twenty-fourth floor, so he asked Patrick to "guard" them while he ran back for the keys. Mike felt a little uneasy leaving his young son in the middle of a Las Vegas parking lot, but it was midday, and he would only be gone ten minutes.

A sinner can repent but stupid is forever.

BILLY SUNDAY

When he reached the hotel room, Nicole asked where Patrick was.

Mike pointed to the window. "He's down there with the car and luggage."

"He's what?" Nicole's eyes widened and she spun around to face him.

Oh, no. I'm in trouble now. Mike winced and repeated what he had said.

"Are you crazy?" Nicole screamed. "You left our 'baby' alone in a Las Vegas parking lot?"

Mike bolted to the elevator, fearing the worst. His only son—kidnapped in Sin City, never to be seen again. When he reached the car, Patrick was standing with his hands in his pockets.

Mike hugged him, threw the bags in the car, and escorted Patrick back to the hotel room. Then he sat him down on the queen bed and looked him squarely in the eyes. Mike wasn't relishing the opportunity to admit that he had blown it, especially in front of his family, but he knew this was a significant moment.

"Patrick, Daddy just did a really foolish thing. I left you out with the car all alone, and I shouldn't have. I made a big mistake. I'm sorry, and I won't let it happen again. Can you forgive me?"

Patrick cast his eyes downward and whispered, "Sure, Dad. It's okay." Then he jumped up and gave his dad a big hug.

Mike had never felt so thankful in his life. Not only was his son safe, but he had experienced the unconditional love of a child.

Later that night when Mike had a chance to be alone with the Lord, he felt God whispering to his heart. *Mike, you've done some foolish things in life and leaving your son in the parking lot took the cake. But just as Patrick forgave you today, so I have forgiven you for all the times in the past when you've hurt me, for all the foolish things you've ever done. And remember, Mike, you may fail and disappoint Me, but I will never fail or disappoint you.*

Mike knew he'd been given a rare glimpse of what God's unconditional love is all about.

The nineteenth-century lamp stood proudly on the living room end table, a crown jewel in an otherwise plain household. To Jack Wagoner, it was a precious pearl—the one priceless object in a home of hand-me-down furnishings.

The lamp had been passed down through the Wagoner family for generations. Before the turn of the century, it had been an oil lamp, sporting a large aqua crystal-ball globe and a gold-painted ornamental steel base. At some point, a family member had adapted it to electricity. Jack took great pride in showing the lamp to all his visitors, carefully detailing its long family history. The lamp not only lit their home, it also brought light to his heart.

One day while Jack was at work, his two young sons were roughhousing in the family living room. One was the cowboy, and the other a bucking bronco. Cowboys have ropes, you know, so to tame this wild bronco, the cowboy lassoed the bronco. Then he tied the steed to the tall end table that displayed the Wagoner family lamp.

Mercy imitates God and disappoints Satan.

JOHN CHRYSOSTOM

The bronco reared. The rope grew taut. The table tipped over, and the priceless heirloom came crashing to the floor. Instantly, the brothers started to cry. They had broken their dad's most precious possession.

With tears in her eyes, Mrs. Wagoner cleaned up the broken pieces. She tenderly put the large shards of broken glass and the crinkled lampshade in a box, as if somehow God might put it back together through the skilled hands of a miracle craftsman. But that would never happen. You can't glue together slivers of glass.

The boys' anguish turned to fear as their mother scolded them for their carelessness and warned them of the consequences when Dad got home. They fled to their bedroom, wishing over and over that they could turn back the clock and make the lamp whole again.

When Jack walked through the front door, his wife told him about the terrible accident. Upstairs, he found the boys cowering in the bedroom they shared.

"I didn't mean to do it, Dad," Tom wailed. "I'm sorry, I really am." Then he turned away to receive his well-deserved punishment.

But instead of a spanking, Jack wrapped his gentle arms around the boy.

"Tom," he said in a sad, soft voice, "I'm not going to spank you or your brother. Your mother told me it was an accident."

"But I broke the lamp," Tom sobbed. "It's ruined."

"Yes, it's ruined," said Jack softly, "but it's just a lamp. Someday, a long time from now, you may have a son or even a grandson. He may break something that's very important to you, and when that happens, I want you to remember this day. I want you to know that he didn't mean to hurt you. He'll love you, just as I love you." Jack hugged both of his sons and walked out of the room.

He had lost a valued heirloom but had gained something even more precious: The opportunity to show his sons that they were far more precious than any physical possession, even the family lamp.

He also heard God whisper in his heart that a father's love and forgiveness are far greater than the value of any possession.

And Jack listened.

et's face it. Although we deceive ourselves into thinking we're quite visionary, our culture is actually very shortsighted. Especially in the area of financial planning.

Now there's nothing wrong with financial planning; in fact, the Scriptures encourage it. But so much of modern-day financial planning is incredibly shortsighted.

In a nutshell, the two big issues of financial planning are getting your kids through college and financing your retirement.

If you have young children, no doubt you've read about the rising costs of a college education According to the latest statistics, by the time your five-year-old is ready to enter college, it will cost $48,000 just for the meal plan.

The other issue of financial planning is saving enough to enjoy your current lifestyle when you retire. And when you put a pencil to it, you discover that you need to be saving something like $9000 a month to do that.

I've obviously exaggerated the case, but the point is this. Somehow, with the Lord's help, we get our kids through college. And somehow, with good planning and His provision, He'll take care of us when we reach old age.

But then you we're going to die. And then what are we going to do?

You see when you die, Keoughs and 401Ks and Roth IRAs aren't relevant. You're going to need some other kind of security.

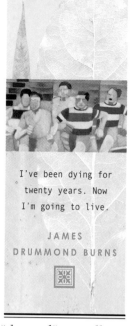

I've been dying for twenty years. Now I'm going to live.

JAMES
DRUMMOND BURNS

If you weren't going to die, you could just keep socking money away in your retirement portfolio. But you *are* going to die. So to put a lot of energy and effort into planning for retirement and not put any thought into what you're going to do with eternity after you die doesn't make much sense.

And you will continue to live after you die. That's what the Bible clearly teaches. So "the end" is really just a beginning.

What kind of planning have you done for eternity? Jesus Christ came to this earth, lived a sinless life, and died on a cross to pay for the guilt of our sins. Some men are trying to earn their way to heaven by good works, but that's crazy. You have a better chance of paying the national debt than you do of earning God's forgiveness. He requires 100 percent perfection! That means you and I come up short.

But Jesus Christ paid the debt we could never pay. He made it possible to have our sins forgiven, to come into relationship with God the Father as one of His children.

Have you come to grips with this issue in your life? Romans 6:23 says that "the wages of sin is death, but the gift of God is eternal life in Christ Jesus our Lord."

Romans 10:9, 10 explains how we can receive this gift of forgiveness in God's sight: "If you confess with your mouth the Lord Jesus and believe in your heart that God has raised Him from the dead, you will be saved."

Have you asked Christ to take away your sins and your failures, and to give you a completely new start? Have you asked Him to take over your life?

If you haven't, open your heart to Him and give Him your life. And once you do that, when you breathe your last breath, it won't be "the end."

It will be the beginning.